Jokes Not To Tell Your Parents

ANSWERS TO
PUZZLES ON
PAGES 92-96

PLINKITY
PLONKITY
PLUNK

HOWARD—
A SIX YEAR OLD
PIANO-PLAYING
BUDGIE

JOKES NOT TO TELL YOUR PARENTS

Gill Brown

Illustrated by David Mostyn

RED FOX

A Red Fox Book

Published by Random Century Children's Books
20 Vauxhall Bridge Road, London SW1V 2SA
A division of the Random Century Group

London Melbourne Sydney Auckland
Johannesburg and agencies throughout the world

Red Fox edition 1991

Text © Gill Brown 1991
Illustrations © Oxford Graphics 1991

The right of Gill Brown and David Mostyn to be identified as the
author and illustrator of this work respectively has been asserted by
them in accordance with the Copyright, Designs and Patents Act, 1988.

Set in Century Oldstyle
Typeset by Getset (BTS) Ltd
Printed and bound in Great Britain by
Cox & Wyman Ltd, Reading, Berks.

ISBN 0 09 974950 5

CONTENTS

dedicated to
our mums and
dads

HOW TOUCHING

FATHER: What did you do with that £1 coin I gave you?
KEN: I swallowed it.
FATHER: Swallowed it? Why?
KEN: Because you said it was my lunch money.

FATHER: Do you like moving pictures?
FREDDIE: Oh yes.
FATHER: Will you help me carry some round to our neighbour's, then?

Freddie came home from school groaning and holding his tummy.

'Are you in pain?' asked his mother.

'No, the pain's in me,' replied poor Freddie.

Mrs Swordswallower went to see her son in the army cadet parade. 'Oh look,' she cried, 'our Oswald's the only one in step!'

DEAR LISTENERS, GUESS WHICH ONE IS OSWALD.

MOTHER: Mary, did you fill the pepperpot as I asked you?
MARY: No, Mum. I couldn't get the pepper down the holes.

Why did Kate's Dad plant a row of razor blades next to his potato bed?
He was hoping to grow chips.

What relation is a doormat to a door?
A step-father.

DAD: What happened to that anti-magnetic, waterproof, shockproof, unbreakable watch I gave you? I haven't seen you wearing it recently.
HARRY: No. I lent it to Barry and he lost it.

BATHTIME

Freddie is helping his parents give Cheddar a bath – and what a mess they're all making! Can you see which object (apart from Freddie, his parents and Cheddar) appears in every picture, which object appears in all but one picture, and how many different objects are shown altogether?

WHY?

1. Did Stinker's Dad have to repair the horn on his car?
2. Were Freddie's Dad's socks full of holes?
3. Did Kate's Dad enjoy his job at the blotting-paper factory?

'My Dad's got a job that's easy to stick to.'
'What's that?'
'He works in a glue factory.'

14

15

BEN: Mum! I've just knocked over the ladder against the house wall!

MOTHER: Go and tell your father, Ben, I'm busy.

BEN: He already knows. He's hanging on to the guttering with his fingertips.

MOTHER: What did you learn at school today, Stinker?
STINKER: How to get out of class early by being rude to the teacher.

'My dad has lost all his hair.'
'What made that happen?'
'He spent his life worrying about going bald.'

17

MOTHER: Why are you jumping up and down, Kate?

KATE: Because I just took my cough mixture and I'd forgotten to shake the bottle.

TERENCE – A SMALL RED SNAKE →

I TAKE MEDICINE FOR BALDNESS, BUT IT DOESN'T WORK!

'I can't come to the party. Mum's changed her mind.'

'Is the new one any better?'

TONGUE-TWISTER

Try saying this three times quickly:

Penny's parents' principal ploy for plucking privet was to plump for plucking privet prettily.

PAT: There's someone at the door selling honey.
MUM: Tell them to buzz off.

SCREEN SCENE

In the top picture Freddie, Kate and Stinker are queuing outside the cinema with their parents. In the bottom picture somebody's parents are seen silhouetted against the screen. Whose parents are they?

MOTHER: Henry, dial the police. There's a man downstairs eating my steak and kidney pie.
FATHER: Should I call an ambulance as well?

STINKER: Mum, I've got a new hobby. I've decided to start collecting worms.
MOTHER: What are you going to do with them?
STINKER: Press them.

MOTHER: Have you packed everything for your holiday? Have you remembered your toothbrush and soap?
DENNIS: Toothbrush and soap? I thought we were going on holiday!

KATE: Mum, I'm homesick.
MOTHER: Homesick? But this is your home!
KATE: I know, but I'm sick of it.

23

'My mum says our house is so small we can only drink condensed milk.'

BRIAN: How's your dad's insomnia?
BRENDA: It's worse. Now he can't even get to sleep when it's time to get up.

KATE'S MUM: Is Cheddar a pointer or a setter?
FREDDIE: Neither. He's a disappointer and an upsetter.

STINKER: Did you know there's a star in the sky called the Dog Star?
CHEDDAR: You can't be Sirius!

26

MOTHER: Did you get a haircut, Imran?
IMRAN: Not just one, Mum, I got all of them cut.

What do you need to know to teach Cheddar tricks?
More than Cheddar!

KATE: Mum, which hand should I use to stir my tea?
MOTHER: Neither, use a spoon.

FREDDIE: Why is your hair going grey, Dad?
FATHER: I expect it's because you and your brother are so naughty.
FREDDIE: Gosh, Dad, you must have been really wicked to Grandpa!

NELL'S MUM: Tell me some more gossip about Mr and Mrs Shufflebottom.
DEL'S MUM: I can't. I've already told you more than I've heard myself.

MOTHER: What would you say if I sat down to supper with hands as dirty as yours?
STINKER: I'd be too polite to say anything.

THE SHUFFLEBOTTOM FAMILY

Mr and Mrs Ernest Shufflebottom have four children. Can you spot which ones they are out of the children running in this race?

JIM: The doctor told my dad he must stop playing golf.

TIM: Oh dear. Isn't he very well?

JIM: *He's* healthy enough, but his game is terrible.

'The doctor told my dad he couldn't make any more hair grow on his head, but he might be able to shrink his head to fit the hair he'd got.'

Why did Dennis the Menace push his father into the freezer?
Because he wanted frozen pop.

'Why are your parents always talking in Spanish?'
'They're adopting a Spanish baby and want to
make sure they can talk to it.'

'My father's the meanest man in the world. When
Mum asked him for a fur for her birthday, he
scraped some out of the kettle.'

FREDDIE, STINKER AND KATE: Mummy, will you help us with our game? We're playing at being monkeys in a zoo.
MOTHER: What do you want me to do?
FREDDIE, STINKER AND KATE: Feed us bananas.

WEDDING DAZE

This is a photograph of Kate's parents' wedding day. Which of the negatives is the correct one for the picture?

HOW MANY WORDS?

How many words, of four or more letters, and excluding plurals, can you make out of the letters in PARENTS? Fifteen is average, over twenty is good, over thirty is excellent!

DAD: You shouldn't hit someone when he's down.
STINKER: What do you think I got him down for?

MOTHER: How many times do I have to tell you to keep away from those buns?
FREDDIE: Never again, Mum. I just ate the last one.

JANE: I'm going to buy you a mug decorated with flowers for Christmas.
MUM: But I already have one.
JANE: No you don't, I just dropped it.

A LOAD OF BULL!

Spot the differences between these two pictures of a happy picnic scene!

39

KATE: My mother suffers from a nervous condition.
JIM: What's that?
KATE: Every time she reads my school report she faints.

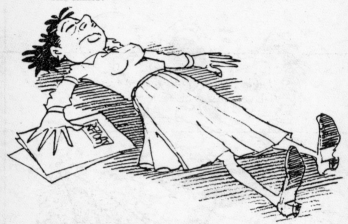

'My dad hates to see my mother digging the garden.'
'What does he do about it?'
'He goes out.'

DAD: Only fools are certain about things. Wise people hesitate.
WINSTON: Are you sure?
DAD: Yes, I'm certain.

FATHER: That record player is driving me mad!
JENNY: I didn't know you needed driving, Dad.

'I didn't know your dad wore a wig.'
'Oh yes. It's an old family hairloom.'

YEP! IT SUITS ME!

PARTY TIME

Kate's parents are having a party, and Kate, Freddie and Stinker are supposed to be helping! Three of the squares that make up this picture are exactly the same. Can you spot which three?

HAND-Y

Try this trick on your mum or dad. Say to them:
'I bet you can't put your left hand where your
right hand can't reach it.' They, of course, will be
sure that they can, and will start stretching their
left hand up in the air and behind their back in the
most peculiar contortions. When they show signs
of giving up, say brightly: 'It's very easy, of
course. *I* can do it.' They won't believe you, but
all you have to do is to put your left hand under
your right elbow and keep it there. There is no
way on earth that your right hand will be able to
reach it!

REALLY WEIRD!

FAMILY GATHERING

Hidden in this word-search puzzle you can find, if you look hard enough, one GRANDAD, one GRANDMA, one GREAT-AUNT, one MOTHER, two FATHERs, four SONs, two DAUGHTERs, two UNCLEs, five AUNTS, one COUSIN, one NEPHEW, three NIECEs, two BROTHERs and two SISTERs. Can you spot them all? The words may read across, up, down or diagonally, either forwards or backwards.

M	N	R	S	B	F	A	D	G	D	B	D
O	I	E	G	A	N	S	D	R	G	R	A
T	E	T	T	U	O	O	A	E	R	O	U
H	C	H	N	N	S	N	D	A	A	T	G
E	E	G	U	T	A	U	N	T	N	H	H
R	L	U	A	N	S	R	A	A	D	E	T
E	C	A	U	E	E	T	R	U	M	R	E
T	N	D	N	H	C	P	G	N	A	E	R
S	U	D	T	H	U	E	H	T	C	T	T
I	C	O	U	S	I	N	I	E	S	S	N
S	R	E	H	T	A	F	I	N	W	I	U
B	T	L	E	L	C	N	U	N	O	S	A

45

STINKER: Mandy's parents are perfectly matched, aren't they?
FREDDIE: They certainly are. She's a pill and he's a headache.

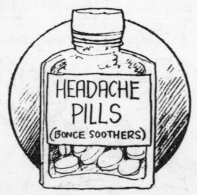

FREDDIE: We got Cheddar for my brother.
KATE: I wish I could do a swop like that with my brother!

NED: Some people *can* cook but they don't.
TED: My dad *can't* cook but he does.

JOE: Is your dad a good cook?
FLO: I don't think so. Yesterday he burnt the salad.

MOTHER: That naughty Cheddar just ate the cake I'd baked for tea!
FREDDIE: Never mind, Mum, we can get another dog.

TEA TABLE

Here is a picture of Stinker's mum setting the table for tea.
Which of the other pictures is the correct mirror image of picture 1?

TERRIBLE
FLYING WEATHER

DAVE: My dad wanted to run his own business really badly.
MAVE: Well, he's realised his ambition. From what I've heard he's a terrible businessman.

'My dad's so fat he can take a shower without getting his feet wet.'

'My mum went on a coconut diet.'
'Did she lose weight?'
'No, but she's very good at climbing trees.'

'*My* mum went on a seafood diet.'
'Did that work?'
'No, every time she sees food she eats it.'

YUM YUM!

ERIC: Your dad is out of this world!
DEREK: My mum wishes he were!

HANNAH: What does Sam's dad do for a living?
ANNA: I think he's a dustman.
HANNAH: I thought he had a certain air about him.

FATHER: You didn't get a very good grade in your exam.
CHEEKY CHARLIE: So what? You don't get very high wages at your job.

55

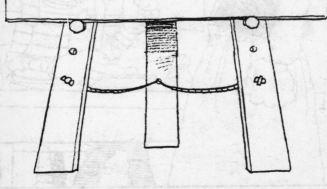

WHERE?

1. Might Freddie's mum find her handbag?
2. Is Kate's dad as beautiful as Kate's mum?
3. Did Stinker's mum keep her piggy bank?
4. Did Freddie's dad wear his old school tie?
5. On Stinker's dad's car are the wheels?
6. Does Freddie's dad wear a buttonhole?
7. Does Freddie's mum keep the chocolate cakes she's baked?
8. Did Stinker's dad take the grandfather clock when one of its hands fell off?
9. Does the grass grow longest in Kate's dad's garden?
10. Might Kate's parents feel cold in midsummer?

NEVER MIND THE ANSWERS AT THE BACK

THESE ARE THE REAL ANSWERS ↓

① £637 REWARD IF YOU FIND IT

② ANYWHERE, YOU SHOULD SEE KATE'S MUM!

③ WITH THE PIG

④ ER... ER... !!!*!?!!*

⑤ STINKER'S dad doesn't have a car

⑥ ~~HERE~~ ANSWERS IN A sealed envelope

⑦ SHE DOESN'T KEEP IT ANYWHERE. FREDDIE SCOFFS IT RIGHT OFF

⑧ THE RIVER

⑨ UNDER his DECKCHAIR

⑩ IN THE DEEPFREEZE

Kate was upset because her doll was broken. 'It's all Freddie's fault,' she cried.

'How did he break it?' asked her mother.

'He jumped out of the way when I threw it at him,' replied Kate.

What's the most worrying thing about being an Egyptian child?
Your daddy might be a mummy.

BARRY: It's true what they say about television being a cause of violence.

LARRY: What makes you say that?

BARRY: Because every time I turn ours on my dad hits me.

When does a father become two fathers?
When he's beside himself with rage.

Stinker came running into the kitchen and asked
for a glass of water.

'Another?' asked his dad. 'I've given you six
already.'

'Yes, dad,' replied Stinker. 'But my bicycle's on
fire.'

'Mum, is it true that before we are born we are dust, and after we are dead we are dust?'

'Yes, dear.'

'Well come quickly, there's someone under my bed and I don't know if he's coming or going.'

HOW WOULD YOU LIKE A POCKET CALCULATOR FOR YOUR BIRTHDAY, SAM?

I DON'T NEED ONE, THANKS, DAD. I KNOW HOW MANY POCKETS I'VE GOT ALREADY.

ON THE WING

Kate's mum keeps budgies and she has let them all out of their cages to fly around the room for exercise. How many budgies can you spot in the picture?

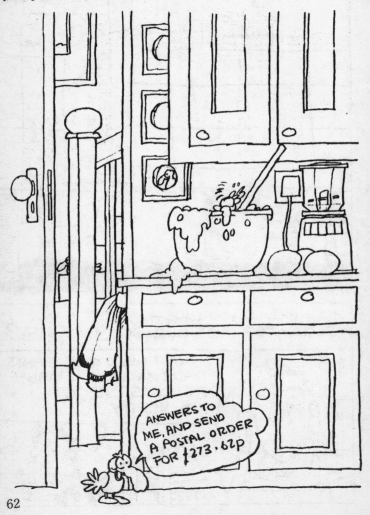

FIND THE NAMES

If the letters of their names are muddled up, Kate's parents are called NALDIBE and TRABMER. Freddie's are called LICERAH and NESHRICTI, and Stinker's RUHART and BANENAL. What are their real names?

TERENCE'S INSTANT ANSWER PANEL

KATE'S PARENTS ARE CALLED —
BLIADNE AND RETBARM

FREDDIE'S PARENTS ARE CALLED
HARLICE AND RICHNESTI

AND STINKER'S ARE CALLED
RATHA-U AND NABNALE

DEEPLY IMPRESSED →

WHAT A BRAIN THAT SNAKE'S GOT

MUM, MUM, DADDY'S GOING OUT!

WELL POUR SOME MORE PETROL ON HIM THEN.

WHAT A FAMILY!

KATE: But Mummy, I don't want to go to America!
MUM: Shut up and keep swimming!

BOO HOO!
(AN HOUR LATER)

Stinker ran into the house in tears.
  'Whatever's the matter?' asked his mother.
  'It's that horrible boy next door,' sobbed Stinker. 'He hit me.'
  'When did he hit you?' asked his mother.
  'About an hour ago,' replied Stinker.
  'But I didn't hear you crying then!'
  'No, I thought you were out,' replied Stinker sadly.

MOTHER: Prakesh! Don't you dare walk on my clean floor with those filthy feet! Take your shoes off immediately!

PRAKESH: But Mum, I'm not wearing any shoes.

IT LOOKS LIKE HE'S NOT WEARING TROUSERS EITHER.

ZONK!

FATHER: And how did the garage window get broken, Darren? Were you playing football near it?

DARREN: No, Dad, I was cleaning my catapult and it went off.

NOBODY UNDER 58 IS ALLOW PAST PAGE 67. ABANDON THIS BOOK NOW AND GO OUT AND BUY "JOKES NOT TO TELL YOUR GRAN, JOKES NOT TO TELL YOUR FRIENDS, AND JOKES NOT TO TELL YOUR TEACHER." ALL, QUITE BRILLIANT. THE GOINGS ON, ON PAGE 68 ARE NOT TO BE ENCOURAGED, IN FACT THEY ARE QUITE DISGUSTING!

SIGNED - HOWIE 'n TERRY

TEA-TIME TROUBLE

Do you ever have boiled eggs for tea? If so, here's a splendid trick you can play on your family.

Offer to get tea ready one day, on your own without any help. You have to prepare for this trick beforehand by saving the empty eggshells from previously eaten boiled eggs. Soak them in warm water while you lay the table, then put them upside down in their eggcups. They will look and feel like the real thing! Then prepare the tea, *using cold water*! Everyone will sit down at the table, ready to enjoy a delicious egg, only to find the shells are empty! They will then pour out cups of cold tea for themselves! Before this happens, it is a good idea if you think of an urgent excuse to leave the room.

SEA-LLY QUESTION

Why wasn't Kate's mum afraid of the sharks when she went swimming in Australia?

KEEP OFF THE GRASS

Who has ridden their bicycle over Kate's parents' lawn? Is it Kate, Freddie, Stinker or one of their friends?

MILLY: A man called to see you while you were out.

FATHER: Did he have a bill?

MILLY: No, just a nose like everybody else.

AS SOON AS I'M OUT OF THIS JOKE — I'LL NIP BACK WITH THE BILL!

Knock, knock.
Who's there?
Fodder.
Fodder who?
Fodder who lives with me and mudder.

MOTHER: Kate's teacher says she should have an encyclopedia.
FATHER: Why can't she walk to school like I did?

MANDY: Why does your Mum put rollers in her hair at night?
ANDY: So she'll wake up curly in the morning.

TEENAGE SON: Dad, may I borrow the car?
DAD: What are your feet for?
TEENAGE SON: One's for the accelerator and one's for the brake.

'Is your dad brave?'
'Brave? When he goes to the dentist they have to give him an anaesthetic to get him in the chair.'

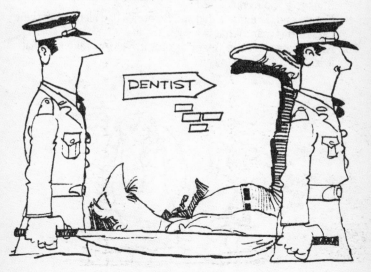

RIDDLES ACROSTIC

Solve the following riddles (all of which are a bit silly) and fit the
answers into the grid. When you have fitted in all the answers you
will find a funny word reading down the arrowed column.

1. What is always dressing in Kate's mum's kitchen?
2. What is all over Stinker's parents' house?
3. Freddie's dad used to be a boxer. What was his favourite
   drink?
4. Stinker's parents took him to the pantomime at Christmas. It
   was the one about a cat in a chemist's shop. What was it
   called?
5. In Freddie's parents' house, this amazing invention lets you
   see through the walls. What is it?
6. If your parents asked you, 'How do you feel?' you might
   cheekily answer like this!
7. What's the first thing everybody's parents do in the
   morning?
8. Kate's parents gave her an apple, but Stinker's parents only
   gave him half an apple. What could Kate's apple do that
   Stinker's apple couldn't?
9. Kate's dad, Freddie's dad and Stinker's dad all take off their
   hats to this man. What is his job?
10. All parents want this, many ask for it, yet few take it. What
    is it?

GROWL!

MY MUM NEVER TAKES IT. SHE DISHES IT OUT!

76

John kept pestering his parents to buy a video, but they said they couldn't afford one. So one day John came home clutching a package containing a brand-new video.

'Wherever did you get the money to pay for that?' asked his father suspiciously.

'It's all right, Dad,' replied John. 'I traded in the television for it.'

I'M GLAD I'M A SNAKE!

MOTHER: Have you been fighting again, Ben? Didn't I tell you to count to ten before you hit someone?

BEN: Yes, but Len's Mum only told him to count to five so he hit me first.

JANE: Have you noticed that your mother smells a bit funny these days?
WAYNE: No. Why?
JANE: Well, your sister told me she was giving her a bottle of toilet water for her birthday.

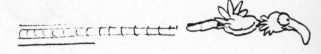

JENNY: Mum, can I have 50p for being good all afternoon?
MOTHER: I suppose so, but I wish you'd be good-for-nothing.

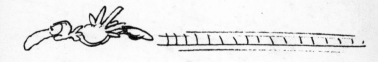

MOTHER: Didn't I tell you to watch when that saucepan of milk boiled over? Look what a mess it's made!
BILL: But I did watch, Mum. It boiled over at quarter past two.

MUM: We're having the Worthingtons for dinner tomorrow.
DAD: Can't we have roast chicken instead?

ANDY: All my friends call me Bighead.
DAD: Don't worry, son, there's nothing in it.

DAD: Do you know this proverb, Mandy? It begins, 'Laugh and the world laughs with you . . .'
MANDY: Mum says it ends, 'Snore and you sleep alone.'

What does a policewoman cook her husband for supper?
I arrest stew.

MUM: There's a beggar outside. Shall I give him one of my apple pies?
DAD: Why – what has he ever done to you?

FREDDIE: Does your Mum cook by gas or electricity?
TEDDIE: I don't know, I've never tried to cook her.

CRACK A CODE

If A = Z, B = Y, C = X, D = W, E = V, F = U, G = T, H = S, I = R, J = Q, K = P, L = O, M = N, N = M, O = L, P = K, Q = J, R = I, S = H, T = G, U = F, V = E, W = D, X = C, Y = B and Z = A, what does the following message mean?

YV   PRMW   GL   NFN   ZMW   WZW

HERE'S ANOTHER CODE — USE IT TO UNDERSTAND THE DEEPLY MEANINGFUL WORDS AT THE END!

A = 1   B = 2   C = 3   D = 4
E = 5   F = 6   G = 7   H = 8
I = 9   J = 10   K = 11   L = 12
M = 13   N = 14   O = 15   P = 16
Q = 17   R = 18   S = 19   T = 20
U = 21   V = 22   W = 23   X = 24
Y = 25   Z = 26

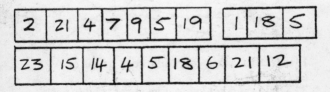

2	21	4	7	9	5	19		1	18	5

23	15	14	4	5	18	6	21	12

MAKE YOUR OWN CODE
AND BE ONE STEP AHEAD
OF YOUR PARENTS.

THIS JOKE IS VERY EMBARRASSING

The old lady outside the school was complaining about the way girls all wore trousers and had their hair cut short these days. 'Look at that girl,' she said, pointing. 'You wouldn't know whether she was a girl or a boy, the way she's dressed.'

'I would,' replied the person next to her, 'because, you see, she's my daughter.'

'Oh dear,' said the old lady, embarrassed, 'I didn't know you were her father.'

'I'm not. I'm her mother.'

ESPECIALLY FOR A SNAKE!

A salesman was trying to persuade a housewife to buy a life assurance policy. 'Just imagine, if your husband were to die,' he said. 'What would you get?'

'Oh, a sheepdog, I think,' replied the wife. 'They're so well behaved.'

I OVERHEARD THAT JOKE!

FUME! STEAM!

84

Who is larger, Mrs Larger or Mrs Larger's baby?
Mrs Larger's baby is just a little Larger.

Knock, knock.
Who's there?
Marmite.
Marmite who?
Ma might, but Pa might not.

GARDEN SIGHS

If Kate's parents' garden measures 24 metres by 12 yards, and Freddie's parents' garden measures 33 yards by 10 metres, whose garden is the larger?

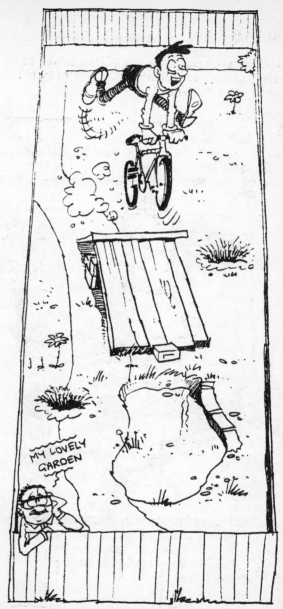

DALEY: We should all help to clean up the environment.
MUM: I quite agree. You can start with your room.

Andy was late for school.

'Andy!' roared his mother. 'Have you got your socks on yet?'

'Yes, Mum,' replied Andy. 'All except one.'

STINKER
NOT
HERE

Stinker and Freddie were discussing their dads.

'Mine's a bit of a magician,' said Stinker.

'How do you mean?' asked Freddie.

'Once he starts waving his magic slipper around, I disappear.'

KATE: May I play the piano, Mum?
MOTHER: Only if you wash those dirty hands first.
KATE: That's all right, Mum, I'll just play the black notes.

'Millicent! What did I say I'd do if I found you with your fingers in the butter again?'
'That's funny, Mum, I can't remember either!'

WE WANT SOME ANSWERS TO THESE JOKES

P. 12/13 Bathtime
*The soap appears in every picture, the bone in all but one picture,
and there are five different objects altogether shown in the pictures.*

P. 14 Why?
1. *Because it didn't give a hoot.*
2. *Because he didn't give a darn.*
3. *Because the work was so absorbing.*

P. 20/21 Screen Scene
Kate's parents.

P. 28/29 The Shufflebottom Family
The Shufflebottom children are numbers 2, 5, 7 and 10.

P. 34/35 Wedding Daze
Negative number 17.

P. 36 How Many Words?
*Here are thirty-six — there may well be more! ASTER, EARN,
NAPE, NEAP, NEAR, NEAT, NEST, PANT, PANE, PARE,
PARSE, PART, PAST, PASTE, PATE, PATER, PEAR,
PERT, PEST, PRATE, RANT, RATE, RENT, REST,
SANE, SEAR, STARE, STEP, STERN, STRAP, TAPE,
TARE, TARN, TEAR, TERN, TRAP.*

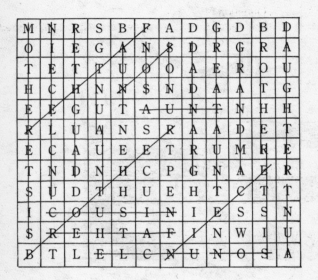

P. 42/43 Party Time
Squares number 2B, 4L and 8G are the same.

P. 45 Family Gathering

M	N	R	S	B	F	A	D	G	D	B	D
O	I	E	G	A	N	S	D	R	G	R	A
T	E	T	T	U	O	O	A	E	R	O	U
H	C	H	N	N	S	N	D	A	A	T	G
E	E	G	U	T	A	U	N	T	N	H	H
R	L	U	A	N	S	R	A	A	D	E	T
E	C	A	U	E	E	T	R	U	M	R	E
T	N	D	N	H	C	P	G	N	A	E	R
S	U	D	T	H	U	E	H	T	C	T	T
I	C	O	U	S	I	N	I	E	S	S	N
S	R	E	H	T	A	F	I	N	W	I	U
B	T	L	E	L	C	N	U	N	O	S	A

P. 50 Tea Table
Picture number 3.

P. 56 Where?
  1. *Where she'd left it.*
  2. *In the dark.*
  3. *She wouldn't say!*
  4. *Round his neck.*
  5. *Underneath.*
  6. *Where he has a button.*
  7. *Away from Freddie and Cheddar!*
  8. *To a second-hand shop.*
  9. *Where it's not cut.*
 10. *In Chile.*

P. 62/63 On the Wing
There are 8 budgies in the picture.

P. 64 Find the Names
Kate's parents are Belinda and Bertram, Freddie's Charlie and Christine, and Stinker's Arthur and Annabel.

P. 70 Sea-lly Question
Because, as she'd heard they were man-eating sharks, she figured they wouldn't attack her.

P. 71 Keep Off the Grass
It was Stinker.

P. 76/77 Riddles Acrostic

P. 82 Crack a Code
Be kind to mum and dad.

P. 86/87 Garden Sighs
Freddie's parents' garden.